The
Betty Booze
Holiday Cocktail Book

Volume 1

Copyright © 2023 by Betty Booze

All rights reserved.

No portion of this book may be reproduced in any form without written permission from the author, except as permitted by U.S. copyright law.

Table of Contents

Holiday Mimosa
Winter Spiced Old Fashioned
Spiced Simple Syrup

White Christmas

Papa's Peppermint White Mocha
White Cranberry Cosmo
Snow White Russian
Coconut Eggnog Martini
Frosted Cranberry Margarita
White Carrot Fizz
Carrot Infused Gin
Spiced Pear Vodka Bellini
Winter Spice Sazerac
Nutty Noel
Almond Joy Martini

Winter Wonderland

Snowflake Martini
Winter Spice Punch
Frosty Pineapple Mojito
Northern Lights
Spiced Cranberry Mule
Frosted Berry Fizz
Icy Peppermint Cocoa
Alpine Cider Hot Toddy
Frosted Gingerbread Latte
Northern Star Espresso Martini

Rustic Farmhouse

Cranberry Rosemary Gin Fizz

Rosemary Simple Syrup
Maple Bourbon Old Fashioned
Spiced Cider Mule
Farmhouse Fig Sour
Fig Simple Syrup
Winter Berry Sangria
Farmhouse Spiced Hot Cocoa
Rosemary Citrus Spritz
Cinnamon Apple Whiskey Sour
Winter Berry Mojito
Chai Spiced Hot Toddy
Chai Spice Simple Syrup

Modern Farmhouse

Grilled Peach Bourbon Smash
Farmhouse Rose Sangria
Roasted Beet Bloody Mary
Dill Pickle Martini
Farm-to-Table Margarita
Forest Floor Martini
Pinecone Punch
Lavender and Juniper Gin Sour
Maple Bourbon Sour
Carrot Ginger Collins
Carrot Ginger Syrup

Fruits and Nature

Pumpkin Spice White Russian
Pumpkin Spice Syrup
Pumpkin Spice Moscow Mule
Cider House Whiskey Sour

Maple Bourbon Sour
Persimmon Smash
Autumn Old Fashioned
Spiced Maple Manhattan
Blackcurrant Gin Fizz
Maple Punch
Christmas Lemon Drop

Chocolate

Chocolate Peanut Butter Cream Martini
Jolly Mudslide
Chocolate Old Fashioned
Cocoa A Trois
Chilled Cocoa Dream
Chocolate Covered Cherry Martini
Chocolate Walnut Highlands
White Chocolate Brandy Bliss
Blackberry Alexander
Chocolate Raspberry Sidecar

Bubbly and Effervescent

Passion Fruit Champagne Cocktail
Gin and Champagne
Sparkling Cranberry Rosé
Pomegranate Prosecco Spritz
Caramel Apple Sparkler
Citrus Champagne Punch
Pear Sangria
Blackberry Champagne Mule
Ginger & Pear Tequila Bellini
Noel 75

Classics

Sazerac
Kir Royal
French 75
Ginger Gin Fizz
Ginger Simple Syrup
Champagne Lemonade
Boulevardier
Zombie
Lavender Bees Knees
Elderflower Champagne Air Mail
Honey Syrup
Sparkling Cucumber Basil Gimlet

Brews and Spirits

Irish Velvet
Ebony and Ivory
Stormy Nights
Brown Ale Gin Shandy
Hoppin' Gin
St. Nick's Little Brother
Vixen's Shandy
The Caboose
A Lump of Coal
The Stocking Stuffer

Tropical Paradise

Hawaiian Holiday Twist
Coquito
Strawberry Kiwi Celebration

Sambuca Delight
Winter Escape Mojito
Mango Daiquiri
Holiday Guava Refresher
Seasonal Alexander Twist
Winter Lychee Elegance
Frosty Banana Cream Martini
Banana Cream

The Nutcracker

Nutcracker Sour
Marzipan Manhattan
Enchanted Snowflake Cocktail
Waltz of the Flowers Collins
Nutcracker Elixir
Tchaikovsky Tea
Rat King Rum Punch
Waltz Waltzer
Snow Queen Spritz
Nutcracker Espresso Martini

Candy Heaven

Candy Cane Martini
Salted Caramel Coffee Martini
Gummy Bear Fizz
Licorice Sour
Butterscotch Martini
Bubblegum Fizz
Sour Patch Margarita
Strawberry Starburst Spritz
Sweet Tart Cocktail

Jellybean Bellini
Jellybean vodka

Christmas in Paris

Vin Chaud (Mulled Wine)
Martini aux Marrons (Chestnut Martini)
Mimosa Parisienne
Chocolat Chaud à la Menthe (Hot Mint Chocolate)
Pommeau Cocktail
Bénédictine Sour
Chaud Lapin (Warm Rabbit)
Cassis Spritzer
Winter Spiced Pear Mule
Frosted Cranberry French 75
Cranberry Syrup

Photo Credits

Bottle in cover image by rawpixel, Freepik.com
Christmas wreath in cover image by pikisuperstar, Freepik.com
Green bow in cover image by kstudio, Pexels.com
Burgundy sequin dress in cover image by freepic.diller, Freepik.com
Christmas tree on title page by pikisuperstar, Freepik.com
Cocktail image on final page by Freepik.com
All other images used in this book are in the public domain

Introduction

When deciding which cocktails to serve, think first of your guest list. A small intimate affair may allow you to make a beverage that is enhanced by presentation, while a jamboree where bodies spill into various rooms may require a large batch, grandma's crystal bowl, and a ladle.

Measurements are written as: **oz** for ounces, **T** for tablespoons, **tsp** for teaspoons, and **c** for cups.

If you don't have the dual cup bar tool known as a jigger, get one. A set of two jiggers will give you the four basic measurements and is more precise than tablespoons and cups. Ideal jiggers are: 1 ½ oz over 1 oz and ¾ oz over ½ oz.

With bar spoons you can make the layered effect in drinks. Insert the spoon into the glass and pour slowly over the back of a spoon to create layers. Make sure you are moving the spoon up as you pour so that the spoon remains on top of the liquid. You can also tilt the glass to get this effect. Pick your poison.

Plain old simple syrup is 1 cup of water and 1 cup of sugar. Stir to dissolve, simmer over medium low heat for 10-15 minutes. Set it aside, let cool before using.

If you have a steam wand for heating up milk, that's awesome. If not, take it slow and low over the stove.

Large volumes of liquid take longer to chill; put punches at the top of to-do lists.

A muddling tool looks like a pestle. To muddle: press, twist, release, and repeat until you can smell the aroma of your ingredients.

When preparing citrus peels for garnish, avoid cutting into the bitter white pith underneath the peel.

Regarding orange, lemon, and lime twists, to express the oils from a citrus peel, hold the peel over the glass with the prepared cocktail and give it a twist. You can also rub the twist along the rim of the glass. Most recipes say to garnish with the twist after expressing.

Herbs are used for garnish to add an aromatic appeal. Keep your sprigs thin.

Taste before you serve. If you don't like it, chances are others won't either.

It's your party, mix it up however you want to. Feel free to craft drinks to your taste and preferences.

Above all, enjoy responsibly. Cheers, Merry Christmas, and Happy Holidays!

Betty Booze

The Aperitif

Cranberry Spritz

2 oz cranberry juice
 1 oz Aperol or Campari
 1 oz dry white vermouth
 Soda water
 Orange twist, for garnish
 <u>For Cocktail</u>
Combine cranberry juice, Aperol or Campari, and vermouth in a glass with ice. Stir well and top with soda water. with an orange twist.

Winter Spice Negroni

1 oz gin
 1 oz sweet vermouth
 1 oz Campari
 ½ oz spiced liqueur (such as cinnamon or cardamom liqueur)
 Orange twist, for garnish
 <u>For Cocktail</u>
Stir gin, sweet vermouth, Campari, and spiced liqueur with ice until chilled. Strain into a glass with ice. Garnish with an orange twist.

Pomegranate Fizz

1½ oz pomegranate juice
 1 oz gin
 ½ oz elderflower liqueur
 ½ oz freshly squeezed lemon juice
 Sparkling wine
 Pomegranate arils, for garnish

<u>For Cocktail</u>

Shake pomegranate juice, gin, elderflower liqueur, and lemon juice with ice. Strain into a glass and top with sparkling wine. Garnish with pomegranate arils (seed pod inside a pomegranate).

Holiday Bellini

2 oz cranberry juice
    1 oz peach liqueur
    Sparkling wine or Prosecco
    Peach, sliced thin for garnish
    <u>For Cocktail</u>

Mix cranberry juice and peach liqueur in a glass. Top with chilled sparkling wine or prosecco. Garnish with a thin slice of peach.

Gingerbread Martini

2 oz vanilla vodka
    1 oz coffee liqueur
    ½ oz gingerbread syrup
    ½ oz cream or half-and-half
    Ground cinnamon, for garnish

Gingerbread Simple Syrup

1 c water
    1 c granulated sugar
    2 T molasses
    1 T fresh ginger, grated or minced
    1 cinnamon stick
    ½ tsp ground cinnamon
    ¼ tsp ground nutmeg
    ¼ tsp ground cloves
    ¼ tsp vanilla extract

<u>For Gingerbread Simple Syrup</u>

In a saucepan, combine water, granulated sugar, and molasses. Stir to dissolve the sugar and molasses. Add the grated or minced fresh ginger, cinnamon stick, ground cinnamon, ground nutmeg, and ground cloves to the saucepan. Place the saucepan over medium heat and bring the mixture to a simmer. Stir occasionally to ensure the flavors are well combined. Once the mixture is simmering, lower the heat and let it gently simmer for about 10-15 minutes. This will allow the flavors to infuse into the syrup. Remove the saucepan from the heat and stir in the vanilla extract. Let the gingerbread syrup cool in the saucepan for a few minutes before straining through a fine-mesh sieve to remove ginger pieces and spices. Transfer the strained syrup to a glass bottle and let it cool.

<u>For Cocktail</u>

Shake vanilla vodka, coffee liqueur, gingerbread syrup, and cream with ice. Strain into a martini glass. Sprinkle ground cinnamon on top for garnish.

Sage Pear Bellini

2 oz pear nectar or puree
1 oz sage-infused simple syrup
Prosecco or sparkling wine
Sage leaf, for garnish

Spiced Pear Puree

2 pears, peeled, pitted, and diced (Red Anjou if available)
¼ c sugar
1-2 T water
½ oz freshly squeezed lemon juice
½ tsp ground cinnamon
½ tsp freshly grated nutmeg

½ tsp ground cloves

½ tsp ground allspice

Sage Simple Syrup

½ c granulated sugar

½ c water

4-5 fresh sage leaves

<u>For Pear Puree</u>

Combine all ingredients in a saucepan and cook over medium low heat until pears begin to break down and spices are fragrant. Transfer to blender or use burr mixer and blend until smooth. Strain through fine mesh sieve and allow to chill.

<u>For Sage Simple Syrup</u>

In a small saucepan, combine sugar, water, and fresh sage leaves. Bring to a simmer over medium heat, stirring until the sugar is dissolved. Remove from heat and let the sage steep for about 15 minutes. Remove sage leaves and let the syrup cool before using.

<u>For Cocktail</u>

Mix pear nectar or puree and sage-infused simple syrup in a glass. Fill the glass about halfway with the pear mixture. Top with chilled Prosecco or sparkling wine. Garnish with a fresh sage leaf.

Lavender Lemon Spritz

2 oz gin

1 oz lavender honey syrup

½ oz freshly squeezed lemon juice

Club soda

Lavender sprig and lemon twist, for garnish

Lavender Honey Syrup

½ c honey

½ c water

2-3 tsp dried lavender

<u>For Lavender Honey Syrup</u>

In a small saucepan, combine honey, water, and dried lavender. Bring to a simmer over medium heat, stirring until the honey is fully dissolved. Remove from heat and let the lavender steep for about 10 minutes. Strain out the lavender and let the syrup cool before using.

<u>For Cocktail</u>

Mix gin, lavender-infused honey syrup, and lemon juice in a glass. Fill the glass with ice and top with club soda. Garnish with a fresh lavender sprig and a lemon twist.

Winter Apple Martini

2 oz vodka

1 oz apple liqueur

½ oz freshly squeezed lemon juice

½ oz cinnamon syrup

Apple, sliced thin for garnish

Cinnamon stick, for garnish

Cinnamon Simple Syrup

½ c granulated sugar

½ c water

2 cinnamon sticks

<u>For Cinnamon Simple Syrup</u>

In a small saucepan, combine sugar, water, and cinnamon sticks. Bring to a simmer over medium heat, stirring until the sugar is dissolved. Remove from heat and let the cinnamon sticks steep for about 15 minutes. Remove the cinnamon sticks and let the syrup cool before using.

<u>For Cocktail</u>

Fill a shaker with ice cubes. Pour in the vodka, apple liqueur, lemon juice, and cinnamon syrup. Shake well until chilled. Strain into a martini glass. Garnish with an apple slice and a cinnamon stick.

Cranberry Moscow Mule

2 oz vodka
1 oz cranberry juice
½ oz freshly squeezed lime juice
Ginger beer
Lime wheel, for garnish
For Cocktail

Fill a copper mug or glass with ice cubes. Pour in the vodka, cranberry juice, and lime juice. Top with ginger beer and stir gently. Garnish with a lime wheel.

Thyme and Cranberry Gin and Tonic

2 oz gin
1 oz cranberry juice
½ oz freshly squeezed lime juice
Tonic water
Fresh thyme sprigs
Lime wheel, for garnish
For Cocktail

In a shaker, combine gin, cranberry juice, and lime juice with a few fresh thyme sprigs. Shake well to infuse the flavors of thyme into the mixture. Strain into glass filled with ice cubes. Top with tonic water to your preferred level of fizziness. Gently stir to combine. Garnish with a sprig of thyme and a lime wheel.

Traditional

Nana's Nog

2 oz dark rum

1 oz brandy or cognac

3 oz eggnog

Freshly grated nutmeg, for garnish

<u>For Cocktail</u>

Fill a shaker with ice cubes. Add the dark rum and brandy to the shaker. Shake gently to chill the spirits. Strain the shaken spirits into a glass. Slowly pour the prepared eggnog over the spirits in the glass. The two will naturally mix as you pour. Sprinkle a pinch of ground nutmeg over the top of the eggnog and serve.

Hot Buttered Rum

2 oz dark rum

1 T unsalted butter, softened

1 T brown sugar

¼ tsp ground cinnamon

¼ tsp ground nutmeg

Pinch of ground cloves

Pinch of salt

Boiling water

Cinnamon stick or freshly grated nutmeg, for garnish

<u>For Cocktail</u>

In a mixing bowl, combine the softened butter, brown sugar, ground cinnamon, ground nutmeg, ground cloves, and a pinch of salt. Mix until well combined and the mixture forms a smooth batter. Choose a heat-resistant glass or mug for serving.

Spoon about 1 to 2 tablespoons of the prepared batter into the bottom of the glass. Pour the dark rum over the batter in the glass. Fill the glass with boiling water, leaving a little space at the top. Stir the mixture well to dissolve the batter and blend the flavors. Garnish with a cinnamon stick or a freshly grated nutmeg and serve.

Spiced Caramel Apple Martini

2 oz apple vodka

1 oz caramel liqueur

½ oz apple cider

¼ oz cinnamon schnapps

Caramel sauce and thinly sliced apple, for garnish

<u>For Cocktail</u>

Drizzle caramel sauce inside a chilled martini glass.

In a shaker, combine apple vodka, caramel liqueur, apple cider, and cinnamon schnapps. Fill the shaker with ice cubes and shake well until chilled. Strain the mixture into the prepared martini glass. Garnish with an apple slice.

Bourbon Cranberry Sour

2 oz bourbon

¾ oz cranberry juice

½ oz freshly squeezed lemon juice

¼ oz simple syrup

Lemon twist, for garnish

<u>For Cocktail</u>

In a shaker, combine bourbon, cranberry juice, lemon juice, and simple syrup. Fill the shaker with ice cubes and shake well until chilled. Strain the mixture into a glass filled with ice. Garnish with lemon twist.

Apple Cider Mule

2 oz vodka
    3 oz apple cider
    ½ oz freshly squeezed lime juice
    Ginger beer
    Apple slice and cinnamon stick, for garnish
    <u>For Cocktail</u>

In a copper mug or glass, combine vodka, apple cider, and lime juice. Fill the glass with ice cubes. Top with ginger beer and gently stir. Garnish with an apple slice and a cinnamon stick.

Christmas Hot Toddy

2 oz bourbon or whiskey
    1 oz honey
    ½ oz freshly squeezed lemon juice
    1 cinnamon stick
    3-4 whole cloves
    1 star anise pod
    Hot water
    Lemon twist, cinnamon stick, star anise, or orange slice, for garnish
    <u>For Cocktail</u>

In a heat-resistant glass or mug, add the bourbon or whiskey, honey, and freshly squeezed lemon juice. Place the cinnamon stick, whole cloves, and star anise pod into the glass. Fill the glass with hot water, leaving some space at the top. Stir the mixture gently to dissolve the honey and combine the flavors. Let the spices infuse for a few minutes, allowing the flavors to meld together. Garnish a lemon twist, cinnamon stick, star anise, or an orange slice, or a combination of your choice.

Tom and Jerry

1 oz dark rum

1 oz brandy or cognac

Hot milk

Batter

3 large eggs, separated

1 c powdered sugar

½ tsp vanilla extract

Pinch of ground nutmeg

Pinch of ground cinnamon

Pinch of ground allspice

For Batter

In a mixing bowl, beat the egg yolks until they are slightly thickened. Gradually add the powdered sugar and continue beating until the mixture is well combined and slightly creamy.

Stir in the vanilla extract, ground nutmeg, ground cinnamon, and ground allspice.

In a separate bowl, beat the egg whites until stiff peaks form. Gently fold the beaten egg whites into the prepared batter until well incorporated.

For Cocktail

In a mug or heat-resistant glass, add spirits, then add a generous scoop (1-2 tablespoons) of the batter mixture. Fill the rest of the glass with hot milk and gently stir to combine. If you feel spicy, garnish with freshly grated nutmeg.

Poinsettia Cocktail

2 oz cranberry juice

1 oz orange liqueur (such as Cointreau or Triple Sec)

Chilled sparkling wine or Champagne

Orange twist, for garnish

<u>For Cocktail</u>

Chill a champagne flute in the refrigerator.

Pour the cranberry juice and orange liqueur into a chilled glass. Slowly fill the rest of the glass with chilled sparkling wine or Champagne. Gently stir the cocktail with a spoon to mix the flavors. Express and garnish with an orange twist.

Holiday Mimosa

1 bottle of sparkling wine or Champagne, chilled (750 ml)
    1 c orange juice, chilled
    ¼ c cranberry juice cocktail, chilled
    Orange slices, for garnish

<u>For Cocktail</u>

Chill the sparkling wine, orange juice, and cranberry juice cocktail in the refrigerator.

In a champagne flute or glass, pour about ⅓ cup of chilled orange juice. Slowly pour about 2 tablespoons of chilled cranberry juice cocktail over the back of a spoon to create a layered effect. The cranberry juice will settle at the bottom of the glass. Gently pour the chilled sparkling wine or Champagne into each glass to fill it up. The bubbles will help mix the juices. Add a thin slice of orange to the rim of each glass and serve.

Winter Spiced Old Fashioned

2 oz bourbon or rye whiskey
    ¼ oz spiced simple syrup
    2 dashes Angostura bitters
    Orange twist, for garnish

Spiced Simple Syrup

½ c granulated sugar
    ½ c water
    2-3 cinnamon sticks
    3-4 whole cloves
    1–2 star anise pods
    Zest of an orange
    <u>For Spiced Simple Syrup</u>

In a small saucepan, combine the sugar, water, cinnamon sticks, cloves, star anise pods, and orange zest. Bring the mixture to a simmer over medium heat, stirring until the sugar is fully dissolved. Let the syrup simmer gently for about 10 minutes to infuse the spices and citrus flavor.

Remove from heat and let the syrup cool. Once cool, strain out the spices and orange peel.

<u>For Cocktail</u>

In a mixing glass, combine the bourbon or rye whiskey, spiced simple syrup, and Angostura bitters. Fill the mixing glass with ice cubes and stir gently for about 30 seconds to chill and dilute the cocktail. Strain the mixture into a glass with a large ice cube. Express and garnish with an orange twist.

White Christmas

Papa's Peppermint White Mocha

2 oz white chocolate liqueur

1 oz peppermint schnapps

1 oz of freshly brewed espresso

1 c hot milk

1-2 T white chocolate syrup

Whipped cream and crushed peppermint candies, for garnish

For Cocktail

In a heat-resistant glass or mug, combine white chocolate liqueur and peppermint schnapps. Add espresso, hot milk, and white chocolate syrup. Top with whipped cream and crushed peppermint candies.

White Cranberry Cosmo

2 oz white cranberry juice

1 oz vodka

½ oz triple sec

½ oz freshly squeezed lime juice

Lime twist, for garnish

For Cocktail

In a shaker, combine white cranberry juice, vodka, triple sec, and lime juice. Fill the shaker with ice cubes and shake well until chilled. Strain the mixture into a chilled martini glass. Express and garnish with lime twist.

Snow White Russian

2 oz vodka

1 oz coffee liqueur (such as Kahlúa)

1 oz coconut milk or coconut cream

Shaved white chocolate, for garnish

<u>For Cocktail</u>

In a glass filled with ice cubes, combine vodka and coffee liqueur. Float the coconut milk or coconut cream on top. Garnish with shaved white chocolate.

Coconut Eggnog Martini

2 oz coconut rum

2 oz coconut milk eggnog

½ oz coconut cream

Freshly grated nutmeg, for garnish

<u>For Cocktail</u>

In a shaker, combine coconut rum, coconut milk eggnog, and coconut cream. Fill the shaker with ice cubes and shake well until chilled. Strain the mixture into a chilled martini glass. Garnish with freshly grated nutmeg.

Frosted Cranberry Margarita

2 oz silver tequila

1 oz cranberry juice

½ oz triple sec

½ oz freshly squeezed lime juice

Rosemary sprig and lime wedge, for garnish

<u>For Cocktail</u>

In a shaker, combine silver tequila, cranberry juice, triple sec, lime juice, and 1-2 rosemary sprigs. Fill the shaker with ice cubes and shake well until chilled. Strain the mixture into a glass filled with ice. Garnish with a rosemary sprig and lime wedge.

White Carrot Fizz

2 oz carrot-infused gin

    ½ oz elderflower liqueur

    ½ oz freshly squeezed lemon juice

    1 oz soda water

    Carrot ribbon, for garnish

Carrot Infused Gin

1 cup gin

    1 white carrot, peeled and sliced thin

    <u>For Carrot Infused Gin</u>

Infuse the gin by placing white carrot slices in a glass jar, then pouring in the gin. Let it sit for a day or two before straining.

    <u>For Cocktail</u>

In a shaker, combine carrot-infused gin, elderflower liqueur, and lemon juice. Fill the shaker with ice cubes and shake well until chilled. Strain the mixture into a glass filled with ice. Top with soda water and gently stir. Garnish with a ribbon of white carrot.

Spiced Pear Vodka Bellini

2 oz vodka (such as Kettle One or Grey Goose)

    1 oz pear puree (see Sage Pear Bellini)

    Chilled sparkling wine or Champagne

    Pear, sliced thin for garnish

    <u>For Cocktail</u>

In a shaker, combine vodka and pear puree and shake to incorporate. Fill a champagne flute halfway with the vodka-peach mixture. Top with chilled sparkling wine or Champagne. Garnish with a thin slice of pear.

Winter Spice Sazerac

2 oz rye whiskey

¼ oz spiced simple syrup (see Winter Spiced Old Fashioned)

2-3 dashes Peychaud's bitters

Absinthe or Herbsaint (for rinsing the glass)

Lemon twist, for garnish

<u>For Cocktail</u>

Chill an Old-Fashioned glass by filling it with ice and setting it aside.

Discard the ice from the chilled glass and rinse it with a small amount of absinthe or Herbsaint. Swirl the liquid around the glass to coat the inside, then discard any excess.

In a mixing glass, combine rye whiskey, spiced simple syrup, and dashes of Peychaud's bitters. Fill the mixing glass with ice cubes and stir well to chill and dilute the mixture. Strain into prepared glass. Express and garnish with a lemon twist.

Nutty Noel

½ oz hazelnut liqueur (such as Frangelico)

1 oz vodka

½ oz chocolate liqueur

1 oz cream or half-and-half

Crushed hazelnuts and chocolate shavings, for garnish

<u>For Cocktail</u>

Rim a chilled martini glass with crushed hazelnuts by dipping the rim in a small amount of hazelnut liqueur and then into the crushed hazelnuts.

In a shaker, combine hazelnut liqueur, vodka, chocolate liqueur, and cream. Fill the shaker with ice cubes and shake well until chilled. Strain the mixture into the prepared martini glass. Garnish with a sprinkle of chocolate shavings on top.

Almond Joy Martini

2 oz rum

1 oz amaretto

2 oz coconut milk or cream

Chocolate syrup

Shredded coconut and chocolate shavings, for garnish

<u>For Cocktail</u>

Drizzle chocolate syrup inside a chilled martini glass, creating a swirling pattern on the sides of the glass.

In a shaker, combine rum, amaretto liqueur, and coconut milk or cream. Fill the shaker with ice cubes and shake well until chilled. Strain the mixture into the prepared martini glass. Garnish with a sprinkle of shredded coconut and chocolate shavings on top.

Winter Wonderland

Snowflake Martini

2 oz vanilla vodka

1 oz white chocolate liqueur

½ oz crème de menthe

½ oz simple syrup

Ice

Shredded coconut, for rim

Edible silver glitter or sugar pearls, for garnish

<u>For Cocktail</u>

Rim a chilled martini glass with shredded coconut.

In a shaker, combine vanilla vodka, white chocolate liqueur, crème de menthe, and simple syrup. Add ice to the shaker and shake well until chilled. Strain the mixture into the prepared martini glass. Garnish with a pinch of edible silver glitter or sugar pearls for a sparkling effect.

Winter Spice Punch

4 c apple cider

2 c cranberry juice

1 c orange juice

1 c spiced rum

½ c cinnamon schnapps

Cinnamon sticks and orange slices, for garnish

<u>For Cocktail</u>

In a punch bowl, combine apple cider, cranberry juice, orange juice, spiced rum, and cinnamon schnapps. Stir to mix the ingredients. Add ice and garnish with cinnamon sticks and orange slices.

Frosty Pineapple Mojito

2 oz white rum

1 oz coconut rum

1 oz pineapple juice

½ oz freshly squeezed lime juice

Fresh mint leaves

Club soda

Pineapple slice and mint sprig, for garnish

<u>For Cocktail</u>

Muddle fresh mint leaves in a glass. Fill the glass with ice cubes. Pour in white rum, coconut rum, pineapple juice, and lime juice. Top with club soda and stir gently. Garnish with a pineapple slice and a sprig of mint.

Northern Lights

2 oz blue curaçao

1 oz vodka

½ oz freshly squeezed lemon juice

Lemon-lime soda

Lemon twist and edible glitter, for garnish

<u>For Cocktail</u>

Fill a glass with ice cubes. Pour in blue curaçao, vodka, and lemon juice. Top with lemon-lime soda. Stir gently to mix. Garnish with a lemon twist and a sprinkle of edible glitter.

Spiced Cranberry Mule

2 oz cranberry vodka

½ oz freshly squeezed lime juice

2-3 oz ginger beer

Lime wedge, for garnish

Cinnamon stick, for stirring

For Cocktail

Fill a copper mug with ice cubes. Pour in cranberry vodka and lime juice. Top with ginger beer and stir with a cinnamon stick. Garnish with a lime wedge.

Frosted Berry Fizz

2 oz berry-flavored vodka

1 oz elderflower liqueur

½ oz freshly squeezed lemon juice

Sparkling water

Blueberries and raspberries, for garnish

For Cocktail

Fill a glass with ice cubes. Pour in berry-flavored vodka, elderflower liqueur, and lemon juice.

Top with sparkling water. Garnish with mixed berries.

Icy Peppermint Cocoa

½ oz peppermint schnapps

1 oz white chocolate liqueur

½ oz crème de cacao

Hot cocoa

Whipped cream and crushed candy cane, for garnish

For Cocktail

Prepare a cup of hot cocoa. Stir in peppermint schnapps, white chocolate liqueur, and crème de cacao. Top with whipped cream and crushed candy cane.

Alpine Cider Hot Toddy

2 oz spiced rum

½ oz honey

1 oz freshly squeezed lemon juice

4 oz hot apple cider

Cinnamon stick and lemon wheel, for garnish

<u>For Cocktail</u>

In a heat-resistant glass or mug, combine spiced rum, honey, and lemon juice. Pour in hot apple cider and stir gently. Garnish with a cinnamon stick and a lemon wheel.

Frosted Gingerbread Latte

½ oz spiced rum

½ oz gingerbread simple syrup (see Gingerbread Martini)

6 oz hot coffee

Whipped cream and ground cinnamon, for garnish

<u>For Cocktail</u>

In a mug, combine spiced rum and gingerbread syrup. Pour in hot coffee and stir. Top with whipped cream and a sprinkle of ground cinnamon.

Northern Star Espresso Martini

½ oz vodka

1 oz coffee liqueur (such as Kahlúa)

½ oz crème de cacao

1 oz freshly brewed espresso, cooled

Chocolate covered coffee beans, for garnish

<u>For Cocktail</u>

Fill a shaker with ice cubes. Pour in vodka, coffee liqueur, crème de cacao, and freshly brewed espresso. Shake well and strain into a chilled martini glass. Garnish with a few chocolate covered coffee beans.

Rustic Farmhouse

Cranberry Rosemary Gin Fizz

2 oz gin
    1 oz cranberry juice
    ½ oz rosemary simple syrup
    ½ oz freshly squeezed lemon juice
    Club soda
    Rosemary, for garnish

Rosemary Simple Syrup

½ c granulated sugar
    ½ c water
    3-4 sprigs of fresh rosemary
    For Rosemary Simple Syrup

In a saucepan, combine sugar, water, and fresh rosemary sprigs. Heat mixture over medium heat until the sugar is dissolved, then let it simmer for a few minutes. Remove from heat and let the rosemary steep for about 15 minutes. Strain and let the syrup cool.

For Cocktail

In a shaker, combine gin, cranberry juice, rosemary simple syrup, and lemon juice. Fill the shaker with ice cubes and shake well until chilled. Strain the mixture into a glass filled with ice. Top with club soda and gently stir. Garnish with a sprig of rosemary.

Maple Bourbon Old Fashioned

2 oz bourbon
    ½ oz pure maple syrup
    2 dashes Angostura bitters
    Orange twist and maraschino cherries, for garnish

<u>For Cocktail</u>

In a mixing glass, combine bourbon, pure maple syrup, and Angostura bitters. Fill the mixing glass with ice cubes and stir gently for about 30 seconds. Strain the mixture into a glass with a large ice cube. Express and garnish with orange twist and Maraschino cherries.

Spiced Cider Mule

2 oz spiced rum

1 oz apple cider

½ oz freshly squeezed lime juice

Ginger beer

Apple slice and cinnamon stick, for garnish

<u>For Cocktail</u>

Fill a copper mug with ice cubes. Pour in spiced rum, apple cider, and lime juice. Top with ginger beer and stir gently. Garnish with a slice of apple and a cinnamon stick.

Farmhouse Fig Sour

2 oz bourbon

1 oz fig-infused simple syrup

¾ oz freshly squeezed lemon juice

Egg white (optional)

Fig, sliced thin for garnish

Fig Simple Syrup

½ c granulated sugar

½ c water

4-5 fresh figs, sliced

<u>For Fig Simple Syrup</u>

In a saucepan, combine sugar, water, and fresh fig slices. Heat mixture over medium heat until the sugar is dissolved, then let it simmer for a few minutes. Remove from heat and let the figs steep for about 15 minutes. Strain and let the syrup cool.

For Cocktail

In a shaker, combine bourbon, fig-infused simple syrup, and lemon juice. If using egg white, add it to the shaker. Dry shake (shake without ice) vigorously to emulsify the egg white. Fill the shaker with ice cubes and shake well until chilled. Strain the mixture into a glass without ice. Garnish with fresh fig slices.

Winter Berry Sangria

1 bottle red wine (such as Cabernet Sauvignon or Merlot)
¼ c brandy
¼ c orange liqueur (such as Cointreau)
1 c cranberry juice
¼ c freshly squeezed orange juice
1-2 tablespoons honey
Mix of cranberries, blackberries, raspberries
Orange slices and cinnamon sticks, for garnish
For Cocktail

In a pitcher, combine red wine, brandy, orange liqueur, cranberry juice, orange juice, and honey. Stir to mix the ingredients. Add mixed berries to the pitcher. Refrigerate the sangria for at least 2 hours to allow the flavors to meld. Serve the sangria over ice and garnish with orange slices and cinnamon sticks.

Farmhouse Spiced Hot Cocoa

2 oz rum
4 oz hot cocoa
Whipped cream
Cinnamon and freshly grated nutmeg, for garnish
For Cocktail

Prepare a cup of hot cocoa. Stir in spiced rum. Top with whipped cream. Sprinkle ground cinnamon and freshly grated nutmeg for garnish.

Rosemary Citrus Spritz

2 oz citrus vodka

½ oz rosemary simple syrup (see Cranberry Rosemary Gin Fizz)

1 oz freshly squeezed grapefruit juice

Club soda

Grapefruit slice and rosemary sprig, for garnish

<u>For Cocktail</u>

In a shaker, combine citrus vodka, rosemary-infused simple syrup, and grapefruit juice. Fill the shaker with ice cubes and shake well until chilled. Strain the mixture into a glass filled with ice. Top with club soda and gently stir. Garnish with a slice of grapefruit and a sprig of rosemary.

Cinnamon Apple Whiskey Sour

2 oz whiskey

1 oz apple cider

¾ oz freshly squeezed lemon juice

½ oz cinnamon simple syrup (see Winter Apple Martini)

Apple slice and cinnamon stick, for garnish

<u>For Cocktail</u>

In a shaker, combine whiskey, apple cider, lemon juice, and cinnamon syrup. Fill the shaker with ice cubes and shake well until chilled. Strain the mixture into a glass with a large ice cube. Garnish with an apple slice and a cinnamon stick.

Winter Berry Mojito

2 oz white rum

1 oz cranberry juice

½ oz freshly squeezed lime juice

1 oz simple syrup

Fresh mint leaves, cranberries, and raspberries

Club soda

Lime wheel and mint sprig, for garnish

<u>For Cocktail</u>

In a glass, muddle fresh mint leaves and berries. Fill the glass with ice cubes. Pour in white rum, cranberry juice, lime juice, and simple syrup. Top with club soda and stir gently. Garnish with a lime wheel and a sprig of mint.

Chai Spiced Hot Toddy

2 oz rum or bourbon

    ¼ oz chai spice simple syrup

    1 black tea bag

    4 oz hot water

    Cinnamon stick, for garnish

Chai Spice Simple Syrup

1 c granulated sugar

    1 c water

    1 cinnamon stick

    6-8 whole cloves

    6-8 green cardamom pods, lightly crushed

    1 small piece of fresh ginger, sliced

    ½ tsp ground nutmeg

    ½ tsp ground ginger

    <u>For Chai Spice Simple Syrup</u>

In a saucepan, combine granulated sugar and water. Add the cinnamon stick, whole cloves, crushed cardamom pods, fresh ginger slices, ground nutmeg, and ground ginger to the saucepan.

Heat the mixture over medium heat, stirring occasionally, until the sugar is fully dissolved. Once the sugar is dissolved, let the mixture simmer gently for about 5-7 minutes, allowing the spices to infuse their flavors into the syrup. Remove the saucepan from the heat and let cool.

<u>For Cocktail</u>

Steep the tea bag in the hot water for a few minutes. Remove the tea bag and stir in simple syrup.

Stir in spiced rum or bourbon. Garnish with cinnamon stick.

Modern Farmhouse

Grilled Peach Bourbon Smash

2 oz bourbon

1 grilled peach, peeled and pitted

½ oz freshly squeezed lemon juice

½ oz honey

Fresh Thyme

Crushed ice

<u>For Cocktail</u>

In a shaker, muddle the grilled peach and a few fresh thyme sprigs. Add bourbon, lemon juice, and honey to the shaker. Fill the shaker with ice cubes and shake well until chilled. Strain the mixture into a glass filled with crushed ice. Garnish with a grilled peach slice and a sprig of fresh thyme.

Farmhouse Rose Sangria

1 bottle rosé wine

¼ c brandy

¼ c elderflower liqueur

1 c mixed berries (strawberries, raspberries, blueberries)

1 orange, sliced thin

Fresh Rosemary

Sparkling water or club soda

Ice cubes

<u>For Cocktail</u>

In a pitcher, combine rosé wine, brandy, elderflower liqueur, mixed berries, orange slices, and 1-2 rosemary sprigs. Stir to mix the ingredients.

Refrigerate the sangria for at least 2 hours to let the flavors meld. To serve, fill glasses with ice cubes and pour in the sangria. Top with a splash of sparkling water or club soda. Garnish with a fresh rosemary sprig.

Roasted Beet Bloody Mary

2 oz vodka

4 oz tomato juice

1 roasted beet, peeled and diced

½ oz freshly squeezed lemon juice

¼ oz Worcestershire sauce

2 dashes hot sauce (adjust to taste)

Salt and pepper

Beet greens, for garnish

Ice cubes

<u>For Cocktail</u>

In a blender, combine roasted beet, vodka, tomato juice, lemon juice, Worcestershire sauce, hot sauce, salt, and pepper. Blend until smooth. Fill a glass with ice cubes and pour in the beet Bloody Mary mix. Stir gently. Garnish with beet greens.

Dill Pickle Martini

2 ½ oz dill pickle vodka

½ oz dry vermouth

Dill pickle brine

Dill pickle, sliced thin for garnish

Cocktail onions, for garnish

<u>For Cocktail</u>

In a mixing glass, combine dill pickle vodka and dry vermouth. Add a splash of dill pickle brine from the pickle jar. Fill the mixing glass with ice cubes and stir gently for about 30 seconds. Strain the mixture into a chilled martini glass. Garnish with thin slices of dill pickle and cocktail onions.

Farm-to-Table Margarita

2 oz tequila

1 oz freshly squeezed lime juice

½ oz honey

½ oz fresh carrot juice

¼ oz ginger liqueur (such as Domaine de Canton)

Carrot ribbon and fresh thyme sprig, for garnish

Ice cubes

For Cocktail

In a shaker, combine tequila, lime juice, honey, fresh carrot juice, and ginger liqueur. Fill the shaker with ice cubes and shake well until chilled. Strain the mixture into a glass filled with ice. Garnish with a carrot ribbon and a sprig of fresh thyme.

Forest Floor Martini

2 oz mushroom-infused vodka

½ oz dry vermouth

Lemon twist and edible flower, for garnish

Mushroom Infused Vodka

1 c vodka

¼ c dried mushrooms or your choice (such as porcini, shiitake, or cremini)

For Mushroom Infused Vodka

In a glass container, combine vodka and dried mushrooms. Seal the container and let it infuse for at least 2 days, shaking occasionally. Strain the vodka to remove the mushrooms.

For Cocktail

In a mixing glass, combine mushroom-infused vodka and dry vermouth. Fill the mixing glass with ice cubes and stir gently for about 30 seconds. Strain the mixture into a chilled martini glass. Express and garnish with lemon twist. Additionally, garnish with an edible flower.

Pinecone Punch

1 c pineapple juice

½ c cranberry juice

¼ c orange liqueur (such as Cointreau)

¼ c spiced rum

Orange slices, for garnish

Ice cubes

<u>For Cocktail</u>

In a pitcher, combine pineapple juice, cranberry juice, orange liqueur, and spiced rum. Stir to mix the ingredients. Fill glasses with ice cubes and pour in the Pinecone Punch. Garnish with fresh orange slices.

Lavender and Juniper Gin Sour

2 oz gin

¾ oz freshly squeezed lemon juice

½ oz lavender honey syrup (see Lavender Lemon Spritz)

¼ oz juniper liqueur

Lavender sprig and lemon twist, for garnish

<u>For Cocktail</u>

In a shaker, combine gin, lemon juice, lavender-infused simple syrup, and juniper liqueur. Fill the shaker with ice cubes and shake well until chilled. Strain the mixture into a glass with a large ice cube. Garnish with a lavender sprig and a lemon twist.

Maple Bourbon Sour

2 oz bourbon

1 oz freshly squeezed lemon juice

½ oz pure maple syrup

1 egg white (optional)

Freshly grated nutmeg, for garnish

<u>For Cocktail</u>

In a shaker, combine bourbon, lemon juice, and pure maple syrup. If using egg white, add it to the shaker. Dry shake (shake without ice) vigorously to emulsify the egg white. Fill the shaker with ice cubes and shake well until chilled. Strain the mixture into a glass without ice. Garnish with freshly grated nutmeg.

Carrot Ginger Collins

2 oz gin

1 oz freshly squeezed lemon juice

¾ oz carrot ginger syrup

Club soda

Carrot ribbon and crystallized ginger, for garnish

Carrot Ginger Syrup

½ c granulated sugar

½ c water

1 medium carrot, peeled and chopped

1 small piece of fresh ginger, sliced

<u>For Carrot Ginger Syrup</u>

In a saucepan, combine sugar, water, chopped carrot, and sliced ginger. Heat over medium heat until the sugar is dissolved, then let it simmer for a few minutes. Remove from heat and let the carrot and ginger steep for about 15 minutes. Strain and let the syrup cool.

<u>For Cocktail</u>

In a shaker, combine gin, lemon juice, and carrot ginger syrup. Fill the shaker with ice cubes and shake well until chilled. Strain the mixture into a glass filled with ice. Top with club soda and stir gently. Garnish with a carrot ribbon and a piece of crystallized ginger.

Fruits and Nature

Pumpkin Spice White Russian

1½ oz vodka

½ oz coffee liqueur (such as Kahlúa)

½ oz pumpkin spice syrup

1 oz cream or milk

Pumpkin spice blend, for garnish

Pumpkin Spice Syrup

½ c water

½ c granulated sugar

2 T pumpkin puree

1 tsp pumpkin spice blend

For Pumpkin Spice Syrup

Combine water, granulated sugar, pumpkin puree, and pumpkin spice blend in a saucepan. Heat and stir until sugar is dissolved and mixture appears well combined. Set aside to cool. Strain before using.

For Cocktail

In a shaker, combine vodka, coffee liqueur, pumpkin spice syrup, and cream. Fill the shaker with ice cubes and shake well until chilled. Strain the mixture into a glass filled with ice. Sprinkle pumpkin spice blend on top for garnish.

Pumpkin Spice Moscow Mule

2 oz vodka

1 oz pumpkin spice syrup

½ oz freshly squeezed lime juice

Ginger beer

Lime wedge and cinnamon stick, for garnish

For Cocktail

In a shaker, combine vodka, pumpkin spice syrup, and lime juice. Fill a copper mug with ice cubes. Pour the mixture into the mug. Top with ginger beer and stir gently. Garnish with a lime wedge and a cinnamon stick.

Cider House Whiskey Sour

2 oz whiskey

1 oz apple cider

½ oz freshly squeezed lemon juice

½ oz maple syrup

Apple slice and cinnamon stick, for garnish

For Cocktail

In a shaker, combine whiskey, apple cider, lemon juice, and maple syrup. Fill the shaker with ice cubes and shake until chilled. Strain the mixture into a glass filled with ice. Garnish with an apple slice and a cinnamon stick.

Maple Bourbon Sour

2 oz bourbon

1 oz freshly squeezed lemon juice

½ oz maple syrup

Orange twist and cherry, for garnish

For Cocktail

In a shaker, combine bourbon, lemon juice, and maple syrup. Fill the shaker with ice cubes and shake well until chilled. Strain the mixture into a glass filled with ice. Garnish with an orange twist and a cherry.

Persimmon Smash

2 oz bourbon or whiskey

2-3 ripe persimmons, peeled and diced

½ oz simple syrup

½ oz freshly squeezed lemon juice

Fresh thyme sprig and persimmon slice, for garnish

<u>For Cocktail</u>

In a shaker, muddle diced persimmons with simple syrup and lemon juice. Add bourbon or whiskey and fill the shaker with ice cubes. Shake well until the ingredients are combined. Strain the mixture into a glass filled with ice. Garnish with a fresh thyme sprig and a slice of persimmon.

Autumn Old Fashioned

2 oz bourbon or rye whiskey

¼ oz maple syrup

2 dashes orange bitters

Orange twist and cinnamon stick, for garnish

<u>For Cocktail</u>

In a glass, combine bourbon or rye whiskey, maple syrup, and orange bitters. Fill the glass with ice cubes and stir gently. Garnish with an orange twist and a cinnamon stick.

Spiced Maple Manhattan

2 oz rye whiskey

¾ oz sweet vermouth

½ oz spiced maple syrup

Dash of aromatic bitters

Orange twist, for garnish

<u>For Cocktail</u>

Chill a cocktail glass.

In a mixing glass, combine rye whiskey, sweet vermouth, spiced maple syrup, and bitters. Fill the mixing glass with ice cubes and stir well.

Strain the mixture into a chilled cocktail glass. Express and garnish with the twist.

Blackcurrant Gin Fizz

1½ oz gin

    ½ oz blackcurrant liqueur

    ½ oz freshly squeezed lemon juice

    ¼ oz simple syrup

    Club soda

    Blackcurrants and lemon wheel, for garnish

    <u>For Cocktail</u>

In a shaker, combine gin, blackcurrant liqueur, lemon juice, and simple syrup. Fill the shaker with ice cubes and shake until chilled. Strain the mixture into a glass filled with ice. Top with club soda and gently stir. Garnish with blackcurrants and a lemon wheel.

Maple Punch

2 oz dark rum

    1 oz apple cider

    ½ oz maple syrup

    ½ oz freshly squeezed lemon juice

    Nutmeg and apple slice, for garnish

    <u>For Cocktail</u>

In a shaker, combine dark rum, apple cider, maple syrup, and lemon juice. Fill the shaker with ice cubes and shake until chilled. Strain the mixture into a glass filled with ice. Garnish with freshly grated nutmeg and an apple slice.

Christmas Lemon Drop

2 oz vodka

1 oz freshly squeezed lemon juice

½ oz cranberry juice

½ oz simple syrup

Sugared rosemary sprig, for garnish

Lemon twist, for garnish

<u>For Sugared Rosemary</u>

Choose fresh rosemary sprigs that are still pliable and not too woody. Wash and thoroughly dry them using a paper towel or a clean kitchen towel. Trim any excess leaves from the bottom of each sprig, leaving a clean stem for holding.

Lightly beat the egg white until frothy. Gently dip each rosemary sprig into the egg white, ensuring it's coated on all sides. Allow any excess egg white to drip off.

Sprinkle superfine or granulated sugar onto a plate. Roll the dipped rosemary sprigs in the sugar, making sure to coat them evenly. You can gently press the sugar onto the rosemary to help it adhere.

Hold each sugared rosemary sprig over the plate and gently shake off any excess sugar. You want a light, even coating of sugar.

Place the sugared rosemary sprigs on a parchment paper-lined tray or wire rack to dry. Let them sit for several hours or overnight. This allows the egg white and sugar to set and create a crisp sugared coating.

Once the sugared rosemary is fully dry, store in an airtight container in a cool, dry place until you're ready to use it.

<u>For Cocktail</u>

Rim a chilled glass with sugar by dipping the rim in lemon juice and then into sugar.

In a shaker, combine vodka, lemon juice, cranberry juice, and simple syrup. Fill the shaker with ice cubes and shake until chilled. Strain the mixture into the prepared glass. Garnish with a sugared rosemary sprig and a lemon twist.

Chocolate

Chocolate Peanut Butter Cream Martini

1½ oz chocolate vodka

1 oz peanut butter cream liqueur (such as Skatterbrain)

½ oz chocolate liqueur

1 oz cream or half-and-half

Chocolate shavings, for garnish

<u>For Cocktail</u>

In a shaker, combine chocolate vodka, peanut butter cream liqueur, chocolate liqueur, and cream. Shake until chilled. Strain the mixture into a martini glass. Garnish with chocolate shavings.

Jolly Mudslide

1½ oz vodka

1 oz coffee liqueur

1 oz Irish cream liqueur

1 oz chocolate syrup

Chocolate drizzle, for garnish

<u>For Cocktail</u>

Swirl chocolate around the inside of the glass.

In a shaker, combine vodka, coffee liqueur, Irish cream liqueur, and chocolate syrup. Add ice and shake until chilled. Strain the mixture into the prepared glass and top with ice.

Chocolate Old Fashioned

2 oz bourbon

¼ oz chocolate liqueur

2 dashes chocolate bitters

Orange twist, for garnish

<u>For Cocktail</u>

In a mixing glass, combine bourbon, chocolate liqueur, and chocolate bitters. Add ice and stir well. Strain the mixture into a cocktail glass. Express and garnish with the orange twist.

Cocoa A Trois

1 oz chocolate liqueur

1 oz hazelnut liqueur

1½ oz Irish cream liqueur

Chocolate shavings, for garnish

<u>For Cocktail</u>

In a shaker, combine chocolate liqueur, hazelnut liqueur, and Irish cream liqueur. Add ice and shake until chilled. Strain the mixture into a glass. Top with whipped cream and chocolate shavings.

Chilled Cocoa Dream

1½ oz white chocolate liqueur

1 oz chocolate vodka

½ oz cream or half-and-half

Chocolate syrup swirl

Instructions:

<u>For Cocktail</u>

Swirl chocolate syrup inside a chilled glass.

In a shaker, combine white chocolate liqueur, chocolate vodka, and cream. Add ice and shake until chilled. Strain the mixture into the prepared glass.

Chocolate Covered Cherry Martini

1½ oz cherry vodka or 1 oz vodka and ½ oz cherry liqueur

1 oz chocolate liqueur
½ oz amaretto liqueur
1 oz cream or half-and-half
Maraschino cherry and chocolate shavings, for garnish
<u>For Cocktail</u>
In a shaker, combine cherry vodka, chocolate liqueur, amaretto liqueur, and cream. Add ice and shake until chilled. Strain the mixture into a martini glass. Garnish with a maraschino cherry and chocolate shavings.

Chocolate Walnut Highlands

2 oz Scotch whisky
2-3 dashes of walnut bitters
½ oz chocolate liqueur
Orange twist, for garnish
<u>For Cocktail</u>
In a mixing glass, combine Scotch whisky, walnut bitters, and chocolate liqueur. Add ice and stir to chill and mix the ingredients. Strain the mixture into a cocktail glass filled with ice. Express and garnish with the orange twist.

White Chocolate Brandy Bliss

1 oz white chocolate liqueur
1 oz brandy
½ oz vanilla vodka
½ oz cream or half-and-half
White chocolate shavings, for garnish
<u>For Cocktail</u>
In a shaker, combine white chocolate liqueur, brandy, vanilla vodka, and cream. Add ice and shake until chilled. Strain the mixture into a glass filled with ice. Garnish with white chocolate shavings on top.

Blackberry Alexander

1½ oz dark crème de cacao

1½ oz blackberry liqueur

1 oz cream or half-and-half

Blackberry and dark chocolate shavings, for garnish

For Cocktail

In a shaker, combine dark crème de cacao, blackberry liqueur, and cream. Add ice and shake until chilled. Strain the mixture into a glass. Garnish with a blackberry and a sprinkle of dark chocolate shavings.

Chocolate Raspberry Sidecar

1½ oz cognac or brandy

½ oz dark crème de cacao

½ oz raspberry liqueur

½ oz freshly squeezed lemon juice

Chocolate shavings and raspberry, for garnish

For Cocktail

In a shaker, combine cognac or brandy, dark crème de cacao, raspberry liqueur, and lemon juice. Add ice and shake until chilled. Strain the mixture into a martini glass. Garnish with chocolate shavings and a raspberry

Bubbly and Effervescent

Passion Fruit Champagne Cocktail

1½ oz tequila

1 oz passion fruit juice

½ oz freshly squeezed lime juice

Champagne or sparkling wine

Passion fruit wedge, for garnish

<u>For Cocktail</u>

In a shaker, combine passion fruit juice, lime juice, and tequila. Add ice and shake to chill. Strain the mixture into a champagne flute. Top with champagne or sparkling wine. Garnish with passion fruit wedge.

Gin and Champagne

1 oz gin

½ oz elderflower Liqueur (such as St-Germain)

Champagne or sparkling wine

Lemon twist, for garnish

<u>For Cocktail</u>

In a champagne flute, combine gin and elderflower liqueur. Top with champagne or sparkling wine. Express and garnish with lemon twist.

Sparkling Cranberry Rosé

4 oz rosé

2 oz cranberry juice

1 oz vodka

Club soda or sparkling water

Orange twist, for garnish

<u>For Cocktail</u>

In a glass, combine rosé, cranberry juice, and vodka. Add ice and top with club soda or sparkling water. Express and garnish with orange twist.

Pomegranate Prosecco Spritz

2 oz pomegranate juice
1 oz Aperol
Prosecco
Orange slice or pomegranate arils, for garnish
<u>For Cocktail</u>
Fill a glass with ice, then add pomegranate juice and Aperol. Top with prosecco and gently stir. Garnish with an orange slice or pomegranate arils.

Caramel Apple Sparkler

1 oz apple cider
1 oz rum
½ oz caramel liqueur
Champagne or sparkling wine
Caramel sauce, for garnish
Apple, sliced thin for garnish
<u>For Cocktail</u>
Swirl caramel sauce in a champagne flute.

In the flute, combine apple cider and rum. Top with champagne or sparkling wine. Garnish with an apple slice.

Citrus Champagne Punch

1 c orange juice
½ c pineapple juice
¼ c freshly squeezed lemon juice
¼ c freshly squeezed lime juice

¼ c simple syrup

Champagne or sparkling wine

Orange, lemon, and lime slices, for garnish

<u>For Cocktail</u>

In a punch bowl, combine the citrus juices and simple syrup. Just before serving, add champagne or sparkling wine. Garnish with slices of oranges, lemons, and limes.

Pear Sangria

1 bottle white wine

½ c pear brandy

¼ c honey

2 pears, sliced

Sparkling wine

Thyme sprigs, for garnish

<u>For Cocktail</u>

In a pitcher, combine white wine, pear brandy, honey, and sliced pears. Refrigerate for a few hours to allow flavors to meld. To serve, fill wine glasses halfway with chilled sangria and top with sparkling wine. Garnish with fresh thyme sprigs.

Blackberry Champagne Mule

1 oz vodka

1 oz blackberry liqueur

½ oz freshly squeezed lime juice

Mint leaves

Ginger beer

Champagne or sparkling wine

Blackberries and lime wedge, for garnish

<u>For Cocktail</u>

In a shaker, combine vodka, blackberry liqueur, 2-3 mint leaves, and lime juice. Add ice and shake to mix and chill. Strain into copper mug with ice, then top with equal parts ginger beer and champagne or sparkling wine. Garnish with fresh blackberries, a lime wedge, and a small sprig of mint.

Ginger & Pear Tequila Bellini

2 oz pear juice

½ oz freshly squeezed lime juice

2 oz tequila

½ piece of ginger, peeled

Prosecco or Champagne

Pear, sliced thin for garnish

Lime twist, for garnish

For Cocktail

In a shaker combine pear juice, lime juice, ginger. Muddle ginger then add tequila and ice, shake until chilled. Strain into champagne flute and top with prosecco or champagne. Garnish with pear slice and lime twist.

Noel 75

1½ oz gin

½ oz cranberry juice

½ oz simple syrup

Champagne or sparkling wine

Orange twist, for garnish

For Cocktail

In a shaker, combine gin, cranberry juice, and simple syrup, add ice, and shake until chilled. Strain into a champagne flute and top with champagne or sparkling wine. Express and garnish with an orange twist.

Classics

Sazerac

2 oz rye whiskey or cognac

1 sugar cube

3-4 dashes Peychaud's bitters

Absinthe or Herbsaint

Lemon twist, for garnish

<u>For Cocktail</u>

Chill an Old-Fashioned glass by filling it with ice and setting it aside.

Discard ice and pour a small amount of absinthe or Herbsaint into the chilled glass. Swirl the liquid around the glass to coat the inside, then discard any excess.

Add sugar cube and Peychaud's bitters to shaker and muddle the sugar cube to dissolve and combine it with the bitters. Add ice and the rye whiskey and shake to combine and chill. Strain into prepared glass. Express, then rub the rim of the glass with the peel and garnish.

Kir Royal

4 oz Champagne or sparkling wine

½ oz Crème de Cassis

<u>For Cocktail</u>

Pour Crème de Cassis into a champagne flute. Top with chilled Champagne or sparkling wine. Stir gently and serve.

French 75

1½ oz gin

½ oz freshly squeezed lemon juice

½ oz simple syrup

2 oz Champagne or sparkling wine

Lemon twist, for garnish

<u>For Cocktail</u>

In a shaker, combine gin, lemon juice, and simple syrup. Add ice and shake until chilled. Strain the mixture into a champagne flute. Top with Champagne or sparkling wine. Express and garnish with a lemon twist.

Ginger Gin Fizz

2 oz gin

¾ oz ginger syrup

¾ oz freshly squeezed lemon juice

Club soda

Candied ginger and lemon twist, for garnish

Ginger Simple Syrup

1 c fresh ginger, peeled and sliced or chopped

1 c granulated sugar

1 c water

<u>For Ginger Simple Syrup</u>

In a saucepan, combine the ginger pieces, granulated sugar, and water. Place the saucepan over medium low heat and bring the mixture to a simmer. Stir to dissolve the sugar. Let the mixture simmer for about 15-20 minutes. Set aside and let cool.

<u>For Cocktail</u>

In a shaker, combine gin, ginger syrup, and lemon juice. Add ice and shake until chilled. Strain the mixture into a glass filled with ice. Top with club soda and gently stir. Garnish with candied ginger and a lemon twist.

Champagne Lemonade

1 oz vodka

1 oz freshly squeezed lemon juice

½ oz simple syrup

Champagne or sparkling wine

Lemon slice and fresh mint, for garnish

<u>For Cocktail</u>

In a shaker, combine vodka, lemon juice, and simple syrup. Add ice and shake until chilled. Strain the mixture into a glass filled with ice. Top with champagne or sparkling wine. Garnish with a lemon slice and a sprig of fresh mint.

Boulevardier

1½ oz bourbon

1 oz Campari

1 oz sweet vermouth

Orange twist, for garnish

<u>For Cocktail</u>

In a mixing glass, combine bourbon, Campari, and sweet vermouth. Add ice and stir. Strain the mixture into a glass with a large ice cube. Express and garnish with the orange twist.

Zombie

1½ oz white rum

1½ oz dark rum

1 oz apricot brandy

1 oz freshly squeezed lime juice

1 oz orange juice

1 oz pineapple juice

½ oz grenadine

Dash of bitters

Crushed ice

Cherry and orange slice, for garnish

<u>For Cocktail</u>

In a shaker, combine white rum, dark rum, apricot brandy, lime juice, orange juice, pineapple juice, grenadine, and bitters. Fill a glass with crushed ice. Strain the mixture into the glass. Garnish with a cherry and an orange slice.

Lavender Bees Knees

2 oz gin

¾ oz lavender honey syrup (see Lavender Lemon Spritiz)

¾ oz freshly squeezed lemon juice

Lemon twist, for garnish

<u>For Cocktail</u>

In a shaker, combine gin, lavender-infused honey syrup, and lemon juice. Add ice and shake until chilled. Strain the mixture into a glass filled with ice. Express and garnish with lemon twist.

Elderflower Champagne Air Mail

1½ oz elderflower liqueur (such as St-Germain)

¾ oz honey syrup

½ oz freshly squeezed lemon juice

Champagne or sparkling wine

Fresh cranberries and thyme sprig, for garnish

Honey Syrup

1 c honey

1 c water

<u>For Honey Syrup</u>

Combine honey and water in a saucepan. Place the saucepan over low to medium heat and gently warm the mixture. Stir occasionally to help the honey dissolve in the water. Continue heating and stirring until honey is fully dissolved, about 4-6 minutes. Set aside and let cool.

<u>For Cocktail</u>

In a shaker, combine elderflower liqueur, honey syrup, and lemon juice. Add ice and shake until chilled. Strain the mixture into a flute glass. Top with champagne or sparkling wine. Garnish with a few fresh cranberries and a small sprig of thyme.

Sparkling Cucumber Basil Gimlet

2 oz gin

    ½ oz simple syrup

    ½ oz freshly squeezed lime juice

    3-4 cucumber slices

    Fresh basil leaves

    Club soda

    Cucumber slice and basil sprig, for garnish

    <u>For Cocktail</u>

In a shaker, muddle cucumber slices and basil leaves with simple syrup. Add gin and lime juice to the shaker. Add ice and shake until chilled. Strain the mixture into a glass filled with ice. Top with club soda and gently stir. Garnish with a cucumber slice and a sprig of fresh basil.

Brews and Spirits

Irish Velvet

1½ oz Irish Cream liqueur

½ oz Irish whiskey (such as Jameson)

4 oz stout beer (such as Guinness)

<u>For Cocktail</u>

Fill a glass with ice. Pour in the Irish Cream liqueur and Irish whiskey. Top with stout beer. Gently stir to combine.

Ebony and Ivory

6 oz stout beer

6 oz pale ale or lager

<u>For Cocktail</u>

Fill a pint glass halfway with stout beer. Place an upside-down spoon over the glass and slowly pour the pale ale or lager over the spoon, allowing it to float on top of the stout.

Stormy Nights

2 oz dark rum

¾ oz freshly squeezed lime juice

½ oz simple syrup

4 oz stout beer

Ginger beer

<u>For Cocktail</u>

In a shaker, combine dark rum, lime juice, and simple syrup. Add ice and shake to chill. Strain into a glass filled with ice. Top with stout beer and a splash of ginger beer to taste. Stir gently and serve.

Brown Ale Gin Shandy

1½ oz gin

½ oz freshly squeezed lemon juice

¼ oz simple syrup

Brown ale

Lemon slice, for garnish

<u>For Cocktail</u>

In a shaker, combine the gin, lemon juice, and simple syrup. Add ice and shake to chill. Strain the mixture into a glass filled with ice. Top off the glass with brown ale. Stir gently to mix the ingredients. Garnish with a lemon slice.

Hoppin' Gin

2 oz gin

1 oz orange juice

½ oz simple syrup

Brown Ale

Orange Twist, for garnish

In a shaker, combine the gin, lemon juice, and simple syrup. Add ice shake to chill. Strain the mixture into a chilled glass. Top off the glass with a splash of brown ale. Gently stir to incorporate the ale. Garnish with an orange twist.

St. Nick's Little Brother

2 oz tequila

1oz tomato juice

1 oz freshly squeezed lime juice

3 dashes hot sauce

2 dashes Worcestershire sauce

4 oz pale ale or lager

Tajin or a blend of salt, sugar, and chili powder, for rimming

lime wedge, for garnish

<u>For Cocktail</u>

Rim a chilled glass with Tajin or blend of salt, sugar, and chili powder.

In a shaker, combine tequila, tomato juice, lime juice, hot sauce, and Worcestershire. Add ice and shake to chill. Strain mixture into the prepared glass. Add beer. Stir gently to combine the ingredients. Garnish with a lime wedge.

Vixen's Shandy

2 oz tequila

1 oz grapefruit juice

½ oz freshly squeezed lime juice

½ oz simple syrup

Pale ale

Grapefruit slice, for garnish

<u>For Cocktail</u>

In a shaker, combine tequila, fresh grapefruit juice, lime juice, and simple syrup. Add ice and shake to chill. Strain the mixture into a glass filled with ice. Top off the glass with beer. Stir gently to mix the ingredients. Garnish with a slice of grapefruit.

The Caboose

1½ oz Jägermeister

½ oz orange liqueur (such as Triple Sec or Cointreau)

½ oz freshly squeezed lemon juice

¼ oz simple syrup

Pale ale or lager

Orange twist, for garnish

<u>For Cocktail</u>

In a shaker, combine Jägermeister, orange liqueur, lemon juice, and simple syrup. Add ice and shake to chill. Strain mixture into a glass filled with ice. Top off the glass with beer. Stir gently to incorporate the beer. Garnish with an orange twist.

A Lump of Coal

1 oz whiskey

1 oz pineapple juice

IPA

<u>For Cocktail</u>

In a chilled mug, combine whiskey and pineapple juice. Top with beer, stir gently, and serve.

The Stocking Stuffer

1½ oz spiced rum

1 oz orange juice

1-2 dashes Angostura bitters

Porter (such as Deschutes Black Porter)

Orange twist, for garnish

<u>For Cocktail</u>

In a shaker, combine spiced rum, orange juice, and Angostura bitters. Add ice and shake to chill. Strain into a glass. Top off the glass with beer. Stir gently and garnish with an orange twist.

Tropical Paradise

Hawaiian Holiday Twist

2 oz dark rum

    1 oz pineapple juice

    ½ oz orange Curacao

    ½ oz freshly squeezed lime juice

    ¼ oz orgeat syrup

    Orange wedge, for garnish

    <u>For Cocktail</u>

In a shaker combine dark rum, pineapple juice, orange Curacao, lime juice, and orgeat syrup. Add ice and shake until chilled. Strain mixture into a glass. Garnish with orange wedge.

Coquito

2 oz white rum

    1 oz coconut cream

    1 oz sweetened condensed milk

    1 oz evaporated milk

    ½ oz vanilla syrup

    Sweetened coconut flakes, for rimming

    Ground cinnamon, for garnish

    <u>For Cocktail</u>

Rim glass with sweetened coconut flakes.

In a shaker combine white rum, coconut cream, sweetened condensed milk, evaporated milk, and vanilla syrup. Add ice and shake until chilled. Strain mixture into a glass. Garnish with ground cinnamon.

Strawberry Kiwi Celebration

2 oz vodka
> 1 oz strawberry and kiwi juice
> ¾ oz freshly squeezed lime juice
> ½ oz simple syrup
> Sparkling wine or Prosecco
> Kiwi, sliced thin for garnish
> Strawberries, sliced thin for garnish
> <u>For Cocktail</u>

In a shaker combine vodka, strawberry kiwi juice, lime juice, and simple syrup. Add ice and shake to chill. Top with sparkling wine and Prosecco. Garnish with kiwi and strawberry slices.

Sambuca Delight

1 oz Sambuca
> 2 oz iced tea
> ½ oz orange juice
> ½ oz freshly squeezed lime juice
> ½ oz grenadine
> 2-3 mint leaves
> Prosecco or sparkling wine
> Lime wheel, for garnish
> Mint sprigs, for garnish
> <u>For Cocktail</u>

In shaker combine Sambuca, iced tea, orange juice, lime juice, grenadine, and mint. Muddle mint then add ice and shake to chill. Top with Prosecco or sparkling wine. Garnish with lime wheel and mint sprig.

Winter Escape Mojito

2 oz white rum

1 oz pineapple juice

½ oz freshly squeezed lime juice

½ oz coconut cream

¼ oz simple syrup

4-5 mint leaves

Pineapple wedge, for garnish

Mint sprig, for garnish

<u>For Cocktail</u>

In a shaker combine white rum, pineapple juice, lime juice, coconut cream, and simple syrup. Muddle mint then add ice and shake to chill. Top with Prosecco or sparkling wine. Garnish with lime wheel and mint sprig.

Mango Daiquiri

2 oz dark rum

1 oz mango puree

¾ oz freshly squeezed lime juice

½ oz simple syrup

Mango slice, for garnish

Lime wheel, for garnish

Mango Puree

1-2 mangos, diced

1-2 T water

½ sugar

<u>For Mango Puree</u>

Combine mango, water, and sugar in saucepan. Cook over low heat until mangos begin to break down. Transfer to blender or use burr mixer and blend until smooth. Strain through fine mesh sieve and allow to chill.

<u>For Cocktail</u>

In a shaker combine dark rum, mango puree, lime juice, and simple syrup. Add ice and shake to chill. Strain into glass and garnish with lime wheel.

Holiday Guava Refresher

2 oz gin

1 oz guava juice

¾ oz freshly squeezed lemon juice

½ oz simple syrup

Club Soda

Lemon twist, for garnish

<u>For Cocktail</u>

In a shaker combine gin, guava juice, lemon juice, and simple syrup. Add ice and shake to chill. Strain into glass and top with club soda. Express and garnish with lemon twist.

Seasonal Alexander Twist

2 oz brandy or rum

1 oz banana liqueur

1 oz coconut cream

½ oz chocolate liqueur

Grated nutmeg and shaved coconut, for garnish

<u>For Cocktail</u>

In a shaker combine brandy or rum, banana liqueur, coconut cream, and chocolate liqueur. Add ice and shake to chill. Strain into glass and garnish with grated nutmeg and sweetened or unsweetened shaved coconut.

Winter Lychee Elegance

2 oz vodka

1 oz lychee liqueur

½ oz freshly squeezed lemon juice

¼ oz honey syrup

Lychee, for garnish.

<u>For Cocktail</u>

In a shaker combine vodka, lychee liqueur, lemon juice, and honey syrup. Shake to chill. Strain into glass and garnish with lychee.

Frosty Banana Cream Martini

2 oz vodka

1 oz banana cream

½ oz orange liqueur

½ oz freshly squeezed lemon juice

Ice cubes

Banana slice, for garnish

Banana Cream

4 ripe bananas, peeled and sliced

¼ c heavy cream

2 T unsalted butter

2 T brown sugar

½ tsp ground cinnamon

A pinch of salt

1 tsp pure vanilla extract

<u>For Cocktail</u>

In a shaker combine vodka, banana cream, orange liqueur, and lemon juice. Add ice and shake to chill. Strain into glass and garnish with banana slices.

The Nutcracker

Nutcracker Sour

2 oz bourbon

    1 oz freshly squeezed lemon juice

    ½ oz orgeat syrup

    ¼ oz allspice dram

    1-2 dashes of Angostura bitters

    Grate nutmeg, for garnish

    <u>For Cocktail</u>

In a shaker, combine bourbon, lemon juice, orgeat syrup, allspice dram, and bitters. Add ice and shake to chill. Strain into the prepared glass. Garnish with grated nutmeg.

Marzipan Manhattan

2 oz rye whiskey

    ¾ oz sweet vermouth

    ¼ oz Amaretto

    1-2 dashes aromatic bitters

    Maraschino cherry, for garnish

    <u>For Cocktail</u>

In a shaker, combine whiskey, sweet vermouth, Amaretto, and bitters. Add ice and shake to chill. Strain mixture into a glass. Garnish with Maraschino cherry.

Enchanted Snowflake Cocktail

2 oz vodka

1 oz Blue Curacao

1 oz coconut cream

½ oz freshly squeezed lime juice

Edible glitter, for garnish

<u>For Cocktail</u>

In a shaker, combine vodka, blue Curacao, coconut cream, and lime juice. Add ice and shake to chill. Strain mixture into a glass. Garnish with edible glitter.

Waltz of the Flowers Collins

2 oz gin

1 oz freshly squeezed lemon juice

¾ oz elderflower liqueur

½ oz simple syrup

Club soda

Edible Flower, for garnish

<u>For Cocktail</u>

In a shaker, combine gin, lemon juice, elderflower liqueur, and simple syrup. Add ice and shake to chill. Strain mixture into a glass. Top with club soda. Garnish with an edible flower.

Nutcracker Elixir

1½ oz hazelnut liqueur

1 oz spiced rum

½ oz Amaretto

¾ oz freshly squeezed lemon juice

½ oz simple syrup

Crushed candied walnuts, for rimming

Grated nutmeg, for garnish

<u>For Cocktail</u>

Rim a glass with crushed candied walnuts.

In a shaker, combine hazelnut liqueur, spiced rum, amaretto, lemon juice, and simple syrup. Add ice and shake to chill. Strain into the prepared glass. Garnish with grated nutmeg.

Tchaikovsky Tea

1½ oz spiced rum

1 oz iced tea

½ oz chai spice simple syrup (see Chai Spiced Hot Toddy)

¼ oz freshly squeezed lemon juice

Cinnamon stick and lemon wheel, for garnish

Rat King Rum Punch

2 oz dark rum

1 oz orange juice

¾ oz freshly squeezed lime juice

½ oz falernum

¼ oz grenadine

Pineapple and lime slices, for garnish

<u>For Cocktail</u>

In a shaker combine, dark rum, orange juice, lime juice, falernum, and grenadine. Add ice and shake to chill. Strain mixture into glass. Garnish with pineapple and lime slice.

Waltz Waltzer

2 oz whiskey

1 oz Amaretto

¼ oz simple syrup

Orange twist, for garnish

For Cocktail

In a shaker, combine whiskey, Amaretto, and simple syrup. Add ice and shake to chill. Strain mixture into a glass. Express and garnish with orange twist.

Snow Queen Spritz

2 oz Prosecco or Champagne

1 oz elderflower liqueur

½ oz freshly squeezed lemon juice

Club Soda

Lemon twist, for garnish

For Cocktail

In a glass combine Prosecco or Champagne, elderflower liqueur, and lemon juice. Stir gently to mix. Top with club soda. Express and garnish with lemon twist.

Nutcracker Espresso Martini

1½ oz vodka

1 oz coffee liqueur

½ oz hazelnut liqueur

1 oz espresso, cooled

½ oz of cream or half and half

Chocolate covered coffee beans, for garnish

For Cocktail

In a shaker combine vodka, coffee liqueur, hazelnut liqueur, and espresso. Add ice and shake to chill. Strain into martini glass. Garnish with chocolate covered coffee beans.

Candy Heaven

Candy Cane Martini

2 oz vanilla vodka

1 oz white crème de menthe

½ oz peppermint schnapps

½ oz simple syrup

Crushed candy canes, for rim

Whipped cream and crushed candy cane, for garnish

<u>For Cocktail</u>

Rim a chilled martini glass with crushed candy canes. To do this, wet the rim of the glass with a bit of water or simple syrup, and then dip it into a plate of crushed candy canes.

In a shaker, combine vanilla vodka, white crème de menthe, peppermint schnapps, and simple syrup. Fill the shaker with ice cubes and shake well until the mixture is thoroughly chilled. Strain the cocktail into the prepared martini glass. Top the cocktail with a dollop of whipped cream and garnish with a sprinkle of crushed candy cane.

Salted Caramel Coffee Martini

1½ oz caramel vodka

1 oz coffee liqueur

½ oz salted caramel syrup

1 oz cream or half-and-half

Caramel drizzle and sea salt, for garnish

<u>For Cocktail</u>

In a shaker, combine caramel vodka, coffee liqueur, salted caramel syrup, and cream. Fill the shaker with ice cubes and shake well until chilled. Strain the mixture into a martini glass. Drizzle caramel on top and sprinkle with a pinch of sea salt.

Gummy Bear Fizz

1½ oz vodka

½ oz raspberry liqueur

½ oz freshly squeezed lemon juice

½ oz simple syrup

Club soda

Gummy bears, for garnish

<u>For Cocktail</u>

In a shaker, combine vodka, raspberry liqueur, lemon juice, and simple syrup. Add ice and shake to chill. Strain the mixture into a glass filled with ice. Top off with club soda.

Garnish with a few gummy bears.

Licorice Sour

2 oz anise flavored liqueur (such as Sambuca or Absinthe)

1 oz freshly squeezed lemon juice

¾ oz simple syrup

Licorice stick, for garnish

<u>For Cocktail</u>

In a shaker, combine anise-flavored liqueur, lemon juice, and simple syrup with ice.

Shake well and strain into a glass filled with ice. Garnish with a licorice stick.

Butterscotch Martini

2 oz vanilla vodka

1 oz butterscotch schnapps

½ oz caramel syrup

½ oz half and half

Whipped cream, for garnish
Crushed butterscotch candy, for garnish
<u>For Cocktail</u>
In a shaker combine vanilla vodka, butterscotch schnapps, caramel syrup, and half and half.

Add ice and shake to chill. Strain the mixture into a martini glass. Garnish with a dollop of whipped cream and crushed butterscotch candy.

Bubblegum Fizz

2 oz vodka
¼ oz strawberry simple syrup
¼ oz banana simple syrup
¼ oz cherry simple syrup
Lemon-lime soda
Bubblegum, for garnish
<u>For Cocktail</u>
In a shaker with vodka, strawberry simple syrup, banana simple syrup, and cherry simple syrup. Add ice and shake to chill. Strain the mixture into a glass filled with ice. Top off with lemon-lime soda. Garnish with a piece of bubblegum.

Sour Patch Margarita

2 oz tequila
1 oz freshly squeezed lime juice
½ oz triple sec
½ oz sour mix
Salt and sugar blend, for rimming
Lime Wheel and Sour Patch Candy, for garnish

<u>For Cocktail</u>

Rim a glass with salt and sugar blend.

In a shaker, combine tequila, lime juice, orange liqueur, and sour mix with ice. Shake well and strain into the prepared glass. Garnish with a lime wheel and a few Sour Patch candies.

Strawberry Starburst Spritz

1½ oz vodka

½ oz freshly squeezed lemon juice

½ oz strawberry liqueur

Club soda

Strawberry, sliced thin for garnish

Starburst candy, for garnish

<u>For Cocktail</u>

In a shaker combine vodka, lemon juice, and strawberry liqueur. Add ice and shake to chill.

Strain into a glass filled with ice. Top off with club soda. Garnish with a strawberry slice and a piece of Starburst candy.

Sweet Tart Cocktail

1½ oz citrus-flavored Vodka

½ oz raspberry liqueur

½ oz sweet and sour mix

¼ oz Grenadine

Lemon twist, for garnish

Sweet Tart candy, for garnish

<u>For Cocktail</u>

In a shaker, combine citrus-flavored vodka, raspberry liqueur, sweet and sour mix, and grenadine. Add ice and shake to chill. Strain into a glass filled with ice. Garnish with a lemon twist and a Sweet Tart candy.

Jellybean Bellini

1 oz jellybean vodka
   ½ oz liqueur of your chosen jellybean flavor
   ¼ oz freshly squeezed lemon juice
   Sparkling wine or prosecco
   Skewered jellybeans, for garnish

Jellybean vodka

1 c vodka
   ½ c jellybean of your choice
   For Jellybean Vodka

Fill a mason jar with vodka. Add jellybeans. Seal the jar and let it sit for 24-48 hours, shaking occasionally. Strain the infused vodka to remove the jellybeans.

   For Cocktail

In a shaker, combine jellybean vodka, liqueur, and lemon juice. Add ice and shake to chill.

Strain into a champagne flute. Top off the glass with sparkling wine or prosecco. Garnish with skewed jellybeans.

Christmas in Paris

Vin Chaud (Mulled Wine)

1 bottle of red wine (Bordeaux or Burgundy)

¼ c granulated sugar

1 orange, sliced

5-6 whole cloves

1 cinnamon sticks

1 star anise

¼ tsp ground nutmeg

¼ tsp ground ginger

Garnish with orange slices, cinnamon sticks, or both

For Cocktail

In a pot, combine red wine, sugar, orange slices, cloves, cinnamon stick, and star anise. Heat over low heat, without boiling, to infuse flavors, about 20-30 minutes. Ladle into mugs. Make sure to include orange slices and spices.

Martini aux Marrons (Chestnut Martini)

2 oz chestnut liqueur

1 oz vodka

½ oz cream or half-and-half

Garnish with crushed marron glacé (candied chestnut)

For Cocktail

Fill the shaker with ice cubes and shake well until chilled. Strain the mixture into a martini glass. Garnish with crushed marron glacé.

Mimosa Parisienne

2 oz orange juice

1 oz crème de cassis

4 oz Champagne or sparkling wine

<u>For Cocktail</u>

Pour crème de cassis into a champagne flute. Add orange juice. Top with chilled Champagne or sparkling wine. Stir gently and serve.

Chocolat Chaud à la Menthe (Hot Mint Chocolate)

8 oz milk

2 oz dark chocolate, chopped

1 oz crème de menthe

Whipped cream and chocolate shavings, for garnish

<u>For Cocktail</u>

In a saucepan, heat milk over medium heat until hot but not boiling. Add chopped dark chocolate and stir until melted and well combined. Remove from heat and stir in crème de menthe.

Pour into a mug, top with whipped cream, and sprinkle with chocolate shavings.

Pommeau Cocktail

2 oz Pommeau de Normandie

½ oz calvados

½ oz freshly squeezed lemon juice

¼ oz simple syrup

Apple slice, for garnish

<u>For Cocktail</u>

In a shaker, combine Pommeau de Normandie, calvados, lemon juice, and simple syrup. Fill the shaker with ice cubes and shake well until chilled. Strain the mixture into a glass filled with ice.

Garnish with an apple slice.

Bénédictine Sour

2 oz Bénédictine liqueur

¾ oz freshly squeezed lemon juice

½ oz simple syrup

Lemon twist, for garnish

<u>For Cocktail</u>

In a shaker, combine Bénédictine liqueur, lemon juice, and simple syrup. Fill the shaker with ice cubes and shake well until chilled. Strain the mixture into a glass with a large ice cube. Garnish with a lemon twist.

Chaud Lapin (Warm Rabbit)

1 oz gin

1 oz honey

1 oz freshly squeezed lemon juice

Hot water

Lemon twist, for garnish

<u>For Cocktail</u>

In a mug, combine gin, honey, and lemon juice. Fill the mug with hot water and stir to dissolve the honey. Garnish with a lemon twist.

Cassis Spritzer

2 oz crème de cassis

4 oz sparkling water

Lemon twist, for garnish

<u>For Cocktail</u>

Fill glass with ice. Add crème de cassis. Top with sparkling water. Express and garnish with lemon twist.

Winter Spiced Pear Mule

2 oz spiced pear vodka

½ oz freshly squeezed lime juice

2-3 oz ginger beer

Pear, sliced thin for garnish

Sugared rosemary sprig, for garnish (see Christmas Lemon Drop)

<u>For Cocktail</u>

In a copper mug or glass, combine spiced pear vodka, and lime juice. Fill the glass with ice cubes. Top with ginger beer and gently stir. Garnish with slice of pear and a sugared rosemary sprig.

Frosted Cranberry French 75

1½ oz gin

½ oz freshly squeezed lemon juice

½ oz cranberry syrup

2 oz Champagne or sparkling wine

Lemon twist, for garnish

Cranberry Syrup

1 c fresh or frozen cranberries

1 c granulated sugar

1 c water

<u>For Cranberry Syrup</u>

Prepare the cranberry syrup by combining cranberries, sugar, and water in a saucepan. Heat and stir until the cranberries burst and the sugar dissolves. Strain and let it cool before using.

<u>For Cocktail</u>

In a shaker, combine gin, lemon juice, and cranberry syrup. Fill the shaker with ice cubes and shake well until chilled. Strain the mixture into a champagne flute. Top with Champagne or sparkling wine. Express and garnish with a lemon twist.

CHEERS!

* 9 7 9 8 2 2 3 6 5 9 8 5 3 *